Laurie MacFayden navi
deft wordplay and disar
relationships – those ent
lovers. Her rich imagery, ... with an ability to locate
the extraordinary in the everyday, results in poems that range from playful to poignant as she celebrates the complexities of the human heart. In this debut collection, best friends scream downhill on their ten-speed bikes; a tree planter spells out her lover's name in seedlings; and a mysterious entity steps out of the mist in Stanley Park. The author contemplates how best to seduce Joan of Arc and goes on an abstract-expressionist date with Jackson Pollock. Like the white shirt in the title, these poems are crisp, seductive and a little bit sweaty.

White Shirt

Laurie MacFayden

Frontenac House
Calgary, Alberta

Book and cover design: Epix Design
Cover Image: "Allegra" by Laurie MacFayden
Author photo: Randall Edwards

Library and Archives Canada Cataloguing in Publication

MacFayden, Laurie
White shirt/Laurie MacFayden.

Poems.
ISBN 978-1-897181-40-9

I. Title.

PS8625.F39W55 2010 C811'.6 C2009-907417-6

We acknowledge the support of the Canada Council for the Arts for our publishing program and the support of the Alberta Creative Development Initiative. We also acknowledge the support of The Alberta Foundation for the Arts.

Canada Council for the Arts Conseil des Arts du Canada

Alberta Foundation for the Arts

Printed and bound in Canada
Published by Frontenac House Ltd.
1138 Frontenac Avenue S.W.
Calgary, Alberta, T2T 1B6, Canada
Tel: 403-245-2491 Fax: 403-245-2380
editor@frontenachouse.com www.frontenachouse.com

For Lindy

Acknowledgements

So much depends upon Eunice Scarfe, for SAGA writing allowed and reading aloud. I am grateful to my family and friends for their ongoing love and support. Heartfelt yodels in particular to Cathy Hodgson, Kerry Mulholland and Amy Willans for being enchanting and lovely; to Thomas Trofimuk, Gordon McRae, Randy Edwards, Mark Kozub and Michael Gravel for the Raving Poets experience; to Melanie Little for pointing me in the direction of Frontenac House; to Shelley Bindon for many meaningful literary discussions over far too many beers; to Claire Gummer for enhancing my vocabulary; to Kim Ferris for nagging me to do this for 25 years; and to Lindy Pratch, first reader and beloved travel companion, for everything.

Published works

The poem "Fifteen" appeared in the Spire Poetry Poster, Vol. 2 No. 9, July 2005.
"Something About Us" appeared in The Ontario Poetry Society Chapbook Anthology *Love: The Main Course*, September 2005.
"Why I Moved To Alberta", "Stars" and "Joan of Arc" (Poems de Terre excerpt) appeared in the Edmonton Stroll of Poets Anthology (2004, 2005, 2006).
"Skillet Prayers and Polar Bears" was commissioned for the CBC Poetry Faceoff, 2008.

Laurie MacFayden was a contributor for the launch of Dailyhaiku.org, a website dedicated to haiku. Her work has been performed in Edmonton's Loud & Queer Cabaret.

Audio

"When they Come for Me", Raving Poets podcast, Live at the Kasbar, recorded November 29, 2006; "Five-Hole", recorded February 2007.

Contents

my date with jackson pollock 11
fifteen 15
what's love? 18
stars 20
white shirt 22
dear life 23
when lust and prayer collide 25
five-hole 26
something about us 28
why i moved to alberta 30
my origami heart 31
song for bedtime 32
after the wind 33
you used to call my name 35
does she know (triangle poem) 37
poems de terre 39
stanley park 42
the door no one opened 45
hobo 46
sometimes 47
notebook 49
homo for the holidays 52
those of us 54
corbett hall 56
melanoma 58
indelirium 60
the knowing 62
getting back 64
when they come for me 66
she had a way 69
correction lines 71
where have all the watering holes gone? 73
skillet prayers & polar bears 76

White Shirt

my date with jackson pollock

he's drunk, of course
shows up forty minutes late
endearingly tipsy, but not mean
at my front door
wearing pressed pants
and tidy bowling shirt

i want the spatter! but he's
cleaned himself up
i want loose fields,
vigorous lines, angry smears!
but he offers me
a single
long-stemmed
dot,
beige
on beige

i want group exhibitionism;
he's a one-man show
on this night i want minotaur tango
but his gait is
autumn rhythm and blues

i say i think i want religion
he nods and offers me a smoke
i know i want blue poles
but i get the wooden horse
i tell him i want chaos chaos chaos
a tear falls from his number 2 eye

i tell him i need hard brush strokes
he shows me a varnished fist
i say i want the ritual of light
he gives me a sloppy hooker's green kiss

get that housepaint off my shoe, i scowl.
he denies the accident
fumbles with nails, tacks, buttons,
key, coins, cigarettes,
matches, etc.

he takes me to a movie
buys me popcorn
it is dripping/ not with butter
says i look lovely, pretty
his voice dripping/not with sarcasm
he opens a vein and lunges towards the screen

i say *drip it on me, lover*
drip that cad red lifeblood all over me
all sticky enamel & oil of linseed
& gestalt number minus 23

after the movie
his convertible
en plein air

i go all number 30 on him, mad with desire
i want still life with cad yellow and tooth marks
i want him to go all fauvist on me
i want thrust of sienna, raw and blistered
all of it outside the lines and smouldering
i want to be driven to abstraction,
to a state of perfect random
he whispers *it's all a myth,*
doncha know that by now, baby?
and stares up at orion

and i don't care
i want those genius hands out of his pockets
and into my mouth

i want the right side of his misunderstood brain
on the left side of my pillow,
his blow hole
gulping gasps of gaping twilight

i want the titanium white of him to get caught
in flagrante delicto
dry-humping my bone-black black
i want that irresistible hit of cobalt
to ignite just under my tongue
i want to savour the thin line of burnt noir
he tattooed under my eyelid
and scratched onto my number 7 toenail

finally
we're in his airy studio barn
i expect messy sex
dirty grinding angry scumble
expect him to go all primary colours on me
expect to be thrown down and ravaged right out of the tube
but his pour reveals a surprising
tenderness
bordering on the
mathematical

i expect animal lust
bull warrior grunts
primal and clumsy and, just like that, over
but he goes all calm and delicate on me instead
blend/binds me in pinks and a softer white
wash of robin's egg and ivory soap
dappled morning skies
kindness

he caresses my cheek, kisses my hair
prepares sweet tea with toast
and suddenly it's giverny all over again
much too much like pears at breakfast, mandarins in a bowl
so i dress quickly
demand that he take me home
i need turpentine fumes
scars on the drop sheets
i need his foot heavy on the gas
hairpin turns in the road
and his brother
nervous with lighter fluid
in the backseat

fifteen

in my mind i'm invisible
and you're still my best friend
and we're riding our bikes
to queen's park every single night of summer vacation
watching the cute boys play softball
buying cokes and hostess chips at addie's confectionary

then on we ride
to the government dock
and we're checking out the boats
and we're watching the fishermen cast their lines
watching red and white floats bobbing
along the surface of the water
and we're sailing off to china
and we're gushing about a movie
about love and a dying girl
and never having to say you're sorry
and we're fifteen and we're wishing we were thirty
and kissable

and on we ride
to kempenfelt park
and all that's between us and the lake is one thin line
of railroad track and some weeds
and we're lying on the grass
we're staring at twilight clouds

and we're swinging on the swings
higher, higher
and we're playing with a matchbox jeep
we found discarded in the sand
and we're fifteen wishing we were six
and that summer didn't ever have to end

and we're gazing across the bay
at minet's point and the rocks and the trees
and the boarded-up railway station
england's over there! we both point, and we are laughing
because that's what you used to think
when you were five and not fifteen

now we're talking to some men in muscle shirts
who stopped to ask directions
they're smelling of suntan oil and export As and whiskey
and they're trying to get us to ride in their car
come to a party with us, they smirk,
and *what do you girls like to do*
on a hot summer night at the lake?
and we're pretending we're twenty-one
and that our names are jenny and sally
and we can't stop giggling
when they actually do call me sally
or when they offer us a drink
from the liquor in their back seat

and we're longing to go with them
and we're panicking because we can't
we won't
we never will
we're fifteen
and we're not invisible
but sometimes we wish we were

and we're back on our bikes
riding like the wind
peeling down supertest hill
hoping the brakes on our ten-speeds don't give out
at the bottom
and we're laughing so much
we're skidding, we're spinning, we're laugh-crashing
over the curb

practically peeing our pants, skinning our knees,
picking gravel out of the blood on our shins
looking each other in the eye and grinning

and we're knowing,
guts-swirling, girl magic, deep-down-deep knowing,
without saying *for always and ever*
without a single spoken word
we're just grinning like hell and knowing that, oh man,
we are best friends
we are invisible
we are invincible
we are fifteen

what's love?

what's love?
she doesn't know.
she was born with a heart defect –
cracked and listing slightly to one side.

what's love? she has no idea.
she thought she loved once, but it turned out to be
acid reflux syndrome.

what's love?
she starts a list:
love is a rose (red, pink, sweetheart)
love is blind.
love hurts/ love stinks!
love is all you need.

love is a banded bird
a shipwreck
it's danger, open excavation,
ground under repair.

love is pre-meditated
a ball and chain, a peanut butter sandwich
love is alive and riding the number 9 bus.

if love is a wish list, she ponders,
if love is the everyday
if love is the answer
if love is, truly, what gets us into heaven
where, then, are the love mechanics?
the love maintenance workers?
the midwives of the heart?
where are the love astronomers
the love custodians
the love drum soloists, the love pipefitters?
where are the love-ta-love-ya-baby bakers
and the burn-baby-burn candlestick makers?

what's love?

all she knows for sure is that
love is the bridge
the boat
the water in the well
the heart.
it's the crack in the heart,
the bailing can,
the stolen salt kiss
the boiling point.

love
is
sticky.

it's the rug and the floor
the head and the hat
the hand and the glove
the sock, shoe and foot

it's cinnamon toast
flannel sheets
kitchen dancing
it's ten thousand drums of hope
leading you out of the dark.

what's love?

she hasn't got a clue.
but she's starting to suspect it has more to do with onions
than with diamonds.

stars

at night she would lie in bed
and stare at the moon through her window
willing it to stay in the same place forever
as if she could rearrange the planets
as if she could say *stop* to the heavens
as if she could prevent the earth from turning
as if

at night she would lie in bed
and invent new names for the constellations:
hoopii and *magniva*, *wondrex* and *katronica*
as if she could rewrite the astronomy books
as if she could recalibrate an eclipse
as if she could supplant copernicus and galileo
as if

the summer she turned fourteen she lay in bed convalescing
from a fever that nearly killed her
she recovered
but her parents were never the same
and the moon
the bloodless moon
stayed in the same place

but she, she swashbuckled her way across the night sky
chasing callisto
flirting with casseiopea
crossing swords with orion, dancing on polaris
feeding the big bear

the summer she turned seventeen
she stopped counting the stars

as if

as if she could ever say no to the night
as if she could ever turn her back on that perpetual longing
that endless cacophony
of twinkle

as if

white shirt

didn't see it coming
blindsided by the drag king of romance
she hooks me with a crisp white shirt and levi's
i go weak in the knees from one sultry sideways glance

she leans in close, lookin' way too good and scented so fine
part ralphie lauren and a splash of merlot wine
grabs my hand: *we have to dance*
she tugs my belt/i'm in a trance
she's a sexy honeyboy and i don't stand a chance

my guts are churning/munch's painted scream
my heart's a splattered pollock drip
she is thunder she is steam
her tongue is metal lightning on my lip

and she looks like the best of my ex-lovers
    all rolled into one
and she looks like four aces   a cathedral   quicksilver
and she looks like pewter   justice   indigo
and she smells like vanilla   sandalwood   sweat

and she tastes like juicy fruit gum
and she tastes like hot chocolate with a hint of rum
and there's something about her that i just can't name
like red smarties and halley's comet
    and an outdoor hockey game

and she smiles like *everything i never dared hope for*
and she grooves like stained glass, double latte extra foam
and she moves like san francisco
and she grinds like new orleans
when she whispers, *i hope you have the balls*
    to take me home

dear life

from a night torn mad with longing

this is me, dear life, no longer merely hanging on
or hanging out
but exfoliating   excavating   taking stock
turning over stones
uprooting plants, going deep with the broom in the corners,
even dusting off the piano keys
in search of answers
to the tough questions

like
who am i   why am i here   why do i feel so
empty   pathetic   different   indifferent
will i ever feel complete unafraid unbroken unfettered?
who the hell invented desire?
and, more to the point,
why have i never kissed that girl
on the mouth?

on that lovely, rude,
tasty, mmmmnn-mmmmnn
unconditionally sexy
honeyed
articulate
perpetually grinning
dream-catching
sword-swallowing
abracadabra
misty mountain
state of the union
special delivery
venus rising
take back the night
hallelujah chorus
graham cracker
cinnamon butter

blissed out
burnt caramel
angel dew
sea salt
tickle-between-the-legs
spontaneous combustion
out-of-the-park
grand slam
thieving, lying,
blackberry, sizzleberry
laughing, law-breaking
generous, jealous
curious, bubble-blowing
swimming hole, cake hole
lemon-puckered/ tongue-sucking
mango-sweet, heart-shaped
cherry-stained fairytale
affirmation-murmuring
pinky-swearing
popsicle-licking/socks-off knocking
fire-starting
thirst-quenching
euphoria-inducing
risk-taking
zoom-zoom
wet wet wet
wake the neighbours
unknowable
untameable
unattainable
untouchable
unforgettable
and
completely untrustworthy

mouth

when lust and prayer collide

once i dreamed of becoming medusa's stylist
now all i want is for you, artemis, to be my mid-life crisis
i pretend to be the noble one hand clapping
when all the while it's at your sweet, sweet ass
my clever tongue aches to be lapping
oh, lover, you can be the buddhist nun
if i can be your smoking gun

take me, quake me inside your godless sleazy bars
and i will show you all my secret holy hunting scars
i'll cleave to you in any sacred ritual you like
if you'll ride me, drive me
on the back of your dharma bike

i'll let you pull my (jealous) hair
if you'll let me put my trembling fingers *there*
amazon armour rarely do i doff,
but for you i'll gladly tear this pagan clothing off
we'll quench and clench and spar and feast
we'll scramble the directions and pray to the northeast

and when it all is said and done
oh, lover,
i'll let you be the buddhist nun

five-hole

go five-hole on me, baby
you got the hands, you got the dangle
you got the scintillating point shot
i hear you can wrist it from any angle

go five-hole on me, baby
let me feel your forehand blast
top shelf just leaves me wanting more
i want your booming slapshot and i want it fast

so go five-hole on me, baby
sex me up in vaughn and bauer
deke me out of my CCMs with the swerve of your curve
puck me gently and sideways, like The Flower

go five-hole on me, baby
penetrate my crease with your easton thrust
cross my red line with your misconduct
bring that raw zamboni lust

go five-hole on me, baby
i'm told your sherwood really rocks
don't worry about body contact
you'll get five for biting and an escort to my private box

go five-hole on me, baby
do your pocket rocket proud
we'll show that kid line a thing or two about scoring
your jumbotron's really heating up the crowd

go five-hole on me, baby
shatter the lens on that play-by-play camera
splay my heart all over the visitors' bench
with your savardian spinarama

go five-hole on me, baby
your hat trick has me in my bliss
'cause it's hockey night in canada, sweetheart
and there's nothing hotter
than a cannonating, centre-ice kiss

(for the uninitiated, the hockey term five-hole
refers to the space between the goaltender's legs)

something about us

there's something about wool socks
keys that fit none of your locks
the seams on a baseball
a red canoe

there's something about trains
whistling under a full moon
hugging the fattest tree
dandelions

there's something about the high level bridge
animal totems
strong dark coffee
rivers

there's something about stone circles
free falling
callebaut chocolate
knowing without speaking

you know, don't you? that there's something about
belgian cherry beer
a ratty grey sweatshirt
inhaling colours in the art store, manet vs. monet

there's something about eleven and four
packing for 2012
unconditional everything
a wall of one's own

there's something about fishing without bait
calling me cliff, not knowing that was my dad's name
bellinis at the macdonald
janis joplin

i know we don't talk of these things
but there's something about snowy owls
bicycle grease
sisters being brothers
the ecology of love

why i moved to alberta

because you gave me a single red rose the day we met
because you ironed your shirt for valentine's day
because your beckoning sky was so much higher than mine
because it's a dry cold
because you kicked your dog off the bed
          to make room for me
because you shared your toothbrush
          with a not-so-perfect stranger
because you showed me your tattoo
          but not your vision of god
because you made me popcorn at midnight
because you offered me your flannel pyjamas
because you made me coffee the next morning
          even though you can't stand the stuff
because you said watching me sleep made you cry
because you said you wanted to grow old with me ...
i said yes

because you always had to do the driving
because you decided valentine's day was no big deal
because you started telling me what to wear
          and how to wear it
because you almost hit me once in the kitchen
because you stopped coming home at night
because you refused to explain where you'd been
because you insisted she was just a friend
because i found her letters in your knapsack
because you said you *still* wanted to grow old with me ...
i said no

my origami heart

it is my own fault
i should never have let you
do all the folding

song for bedtime

tonight i lie in ribbons, in roses
tonight i lie in cloak of blue
my original bed was a robin's nest
my original sky was you

tonight i lie in willow, in stone
tonight i lie in field of green
my original bed was stardust
my original breath, the love not seen

my original tongue
did not speak, did not cry
my original feet did not dance
my original eyes
could see nothing but fear
my original heart took no chance

my original hands
held sticks that made fire
my original teeth took the bite
my original bed was the end of desire
extinguished by daybreak's first light

tonight i lie in sadness
tonight i lie alone
my original bed has grown smaller
and no longer warms
my original bones

after the wind

the shrieking wind she welcomed
it drowned out the voices
the noises
the creaking of the walls
the hammering of the expectation
the children

the wind she respected
but after the wind
the silence was
thunderous

after the wind took the roof
broke the boughs
lifted the fence
she wept in relief
hoping this meant an end
to the experiment
the country living
the *let's get back to the land, honey*
nightmare

he wanted to farm
but never took a step off city pavement
until his 30th year
she was born in a corn crib
and hoped never to see another chicken coop
as long as she lived

after the wind dropped pieces
of the neighbours' tool shed onto their veranda
she was certain he would surrender
call it a day
insist on moving back to civilization
and starbucks

but after the wind
he was even more determined
to stay

after the wind
she had no choice
but to answer
with gusts of her own

you used to call my name

you used to call my name
in the dark
in the night
in the dreamtime
in the private blue panic

now you've forgotten
the smell of my neck
the crook of my elbow
the stir of my spoon
the way i fold my newspaper.
when is my birthday?
you don't know me anymore.
perhaps you never did.

and yet i remember you.
your aries brow,
your obsession with maps and clocks
your red doc martens, charming boyish smile
the casual, heart-on-your-sleeve messiness
so meticulously choreographed
... faker!

you used to call my name
with those lying lips –
nibble my toes for days,
suck me dry with that tongue
drink my blood
devour my words ...
eat eat eat away at me

you don't know me anymore
but your tooth marks still scar my skin
my number is still in your speed dial
your old toyota still knows the way to my house

your dog is still infatuated with my crotch
and your wife ...

your wife still thinks i'm the one
who wrecked your marriage

does she know [triangle poem]

does she know
how much i want the voice on the phone
to be you / to be, always, always you
every blessed time it unfaithfully rings
i want it to be you / for me
you / wanting me
want it to be you / not wanting her
not her / it can't be her
i don't want you to be wanting her
when you've got "get over here" on your mind

does she know
i changed my shirt three times tonight
three times, for you / not for her
i dressed myself for you
wanting you to notice me / me, not her
(it is never for her)

and does she know
does she know that i dream of you
i dream of you and the walls come down
and the scorched love in the dreams is an indigo flare
in an unnamed galaxy
where all the signposts lead to sad arcs and drownings

and i wake and die a little,
i wake and i sometimes die a lot
because i'm lying next to someone
who believes i'd never lie about where i go when i dream
and it kills me
because it's not you / wanting me
it's her / not you
and she wants me / to want her
and i want you / i want you
i want you / and to be wanted by you
and you want her
and i don't have a map for any of this

and does she know
do you know
do you know how much this terrifies me
do you know how much i want you?
how much wanting you like this chills me beyond bone
beyond the far side of pretending it's under control
know how much i ache to belong to you,
ache for you not to go home to her
how much i want to not need you like this
how much i want not to live for that one incendiary kiss

does she know
does she know that when i look at you looking at her
i know you will never look at me that way
does she know
how lucky that makes her?

does she know
that in all the fire poems
i'm the one you change your shirt three times for

poems de terre

the surrender diaries, france, 2004

day 1, en route, montreal.
air canada business class lounge, on points.
brushing up on my french: *toilette, bicyclette, c'est domage, fromage*
i ask my *copine* for *une baguette avec frottage ...*
apparently that's only funny the first 10 times.

time is fleeting ... except when your connecting flight
doesn't leave for four hours
and you're surrounded by free beer, wine, gluttony
and newspapers
and the tv channel is for french children
and the kilkenny you tried to make last is already
making your eyelids droop and you check your watch
and you've managed to kill only 17 minutes
and you realize with horror that if you were straight,
these 50-something suits melted to their cell phones
and laptops
would be your singles-ad demographic
so you decide you better have another kilkenny
and keep reminding yourself
that each fallen eyelash, each crying baby
is a poem

day 3, april in paris
da vinci code be damned,
mona is so much more than just a pretty face
and venus, venus, well, when you get your breath back
you pledge that, from now on,
you will always see the whole girl.

your third belgian beer forces the question:
is there such a thing as too much beauty?
after 129 monets, 17 renoirs, 24 cezannes,
28 matisses and 32 chagalls ...

you re-enter the earth's atmosphere
to discover that water lilies
and caillebotte's *raboteurs de parquet*
cannot protect you from the dog shit
on a paris sidewalk.
merde.

day 6, train to dijon
my bed-and-breakfast host
does not approve of this day trip, proclaiming:
there is so much more to france
than mustard!

day 15
if you were here, would you be bored?
would you hate the rothko? deny the pollock,
challenge the matisse,
ridicule the miro?
would we even leave this rented bed?
would we create our own impressionist masterpiece,
rolling around in croissant crumbs, christening the sheets
with chocolatine smears,
feasting at monet's table ...
or would we starve on van gogh's scraps,
guilt burning a hole in our wine-stained rail pass?

day 19
i am on the train now from nice to avignon,
plugged into *jenny sings lenny*, when it hits me:
i think i'm falling in love with joan of arc.
she just may be the ideal woman,
that one i've never been able to find.
strong. independent. feisty. devoted. high-spirited.

woman of conviction; a cross-dresser
who is not afraid of anything. i bet she's a fire sign;
she can certainly take the heat.

warrior novice / does this girl-soldier wear her armour
to bed? i'd like to watch that striptease.

transmigration of his holiness
to her loveliness, her holy grail
and which do you suppose
would be the man between the sheets?
and underneath all that chain mail and holy heat
she's still a girl / still a girl / still just a girl.

how, then, to steal her away? this radiant,
wide-eyed waif, married to god, bride of christ ...
christ was a carpenter. i could be a carpenter;
i'm told i do good work with my hands.

could she be convinced to take a lover?

she comes to me in a flirty french-kissing dream
so i ask her why she did it; why she just let it come,
the torch, the soot, the burn.

with eyes ablaze, she says
i was never afraid
of those boys, those non-believers.
how did i stand it?
you learn to love the flame.

stanley park

i could live in these woods
these trees
these trees
i love these trees, they way they
hum, murmur, weep
they weep and i am convinced it's all for me
the way they bend, softly creak and cry
all for me

i could live in these woods
i love these cedars and i look like i belong
i must look like i belong, two different sets of people
ask me for directions.
three sisters from texas ask me to take their photo
we're enjoying your city, they smile.
oh, it's not my city, i reply. *i am not from this place.*

i do not tell them that the trees call out to me:
finally, child, you have come home.

i step off the seawall to escape the cell phone joggers,
iPod roller-bladers, rent-a-cyclists,
tourists pelting lagoon birds with salted snacks
in ignorant defiance of signs that implore,
in four different languages,
please do not feed the wildlife

i escape into the ferns
the october-crisp leaves
the cool humidity ... it is 16 degrees celsius
and i swear i can see my breath

jagged stumps are all that remain of the seven sisters.
i do not tempt fate. i stay on the tatlow trail
instead of venturing down the one marked "lovers".

(dare i walk there by myself?) and i realize
i want to be uprooted, transplanted
in these woods

i want anonymous tall cedar sex with a stranger
i want the next person i meet on this trail to look at me
with an almost imperceptible knowing,
barely a nod that says yes, yes, you are the one
i have been waiting for
come with me now deeper, deeper
into the soft damp, where we'll be surrounded
by these trees
by crows, raccoons, too many to count
come deeper into these cedars with me
and we'll rub our hungry hands over each other's limbs,
this green heaving wild the only witness
to our clandestine forest fucking

and
from behind a wall of moss
steps a flat chest narrow waist
high cheekbones large hands
confident gait, not quite a swagger but
steady, sure
spritely androgynous and i can't
tell if it's a boy or a girl and it doesn't matter,
he/she is beautiful.

three steps closer and now i see
she is
perfect.
she has known hunger
and she has seen the blue in everything
and my cheek is smashed up against
lichen/creases of bark/spider webs

her mouth roasted chestnut milky-salty
her branches rare twig, gnarly blood-root

our boots make a chwuuck, chwuuck sound
as we pull them out of the swamp muck

her eyes to the ground now,
shy, reluctant to meet mine

her hair suddenly darker, coarser
than i first noticed
and her wings – her wings! – i missed those completely
the first time

she looks skyward
and says *be careful ...*
be careful what you wish for, angel.

you summoned me, i whisper, tilting my head
did i? she leans into my kiss
and suddenly she is on the highest branch
she is in the sky
she is the sky
she is raven

and i
dumbly sated
return to the seawall
humbled by the keening cedars
fed by the wildlife
grateful
and small

the door no one opened

you are the door no one opened
you are the poor pear in eden's feast of apple
you are the one unbroken heart
you are the prayer

you are the daughter of winter
you are the tear in the good linen
you are the low growl in the dog's throat
you are the sun after icarus

you are the red velvet dress
you are the old country road
you are the water in the well
you are the gasoline on the fire

you are the bread
you are the bell
you are the bride's veil
you are the alpha and the omega

you are the wolf
you are the tooth
you are the crow's portrait of the raven
you are not sleeping tonight

you are the dark glasses
you are the ruby ring
you are the highway to nowhere
you are the dirt under your granddad's fingernails

you are the grounded bird
you are the first blank page
you are the voice of eve and ruth and sarah and medusa
you are the one they thought was lost
you are the door no one opened

hobo

you would call me a nobody
i myself prefer the term
emotional vagabond

i am a nobody
and my mother's given up on me
because i'm hopping boxcars
in search of language for the unseen
for another thousand ways
to say the things i was forbidden to say
shut up shut up shut up

my mother would call the train tracks dangerous
but i take comfort in their stretch
their long steel hum,
the way they just go off
towards an ending you cannot see
you know that ultimately
they must come to a halt out there
somewhere on the other side of trestles and tunnels
and the dangers of unmarked crossings

you would call me a drifter
i myself prefer
not to be called

sometimes

sometimes she will close her eyes
and let you cover her with roses
with the last of sorrow
with fishnet stockings
with kisses that taste of cigarettes and regret
with corduroy

this is not a love song.
her heart skin fingertips lungs
slightly swollen belly
and all of the screaming bones
they live in the shadows

her true north
is a blank cheque
an evil twin
twisted sonnet
pearl necklace
a moonless night
zero gravity
scar tissue
salt water

she desires a gemini yes
a secret spy camera, x-ray goggles
some india ink, a sleazy tabloid headline
and an afternoon in the sun in the south of france
with nothing to do but sip absinthe and paint ripe, recalcitrant
cadmium red
on a beautiful blue, blue girl

she wants rowboat love
jungle sex
an end to the sunflower dreams
and a religion that lets people feel good about themselves

she wants to fall in love with the boy inside of you
the sweet, shy boy who lives inside of girls like you
and simply to feel at home in your hands
your sweet, shy hands

but a storm locks in
and the creek bed floods
and things get lost
things get lost
and the couplets aren't rhyming
and your eyes, your eyes are no longer throwing sparks
or reflecting forgiveness

then spring comes and something melts, something melts
inside the red
inside the beautiful blue, blue girl
something melts
and it turns out that sometimes
sometimes
your boyish, paint-spattered
sweet, shy hands
are forgiveness enough

notebook

disclaimer: this notebook is full of jagged holes and has recently been diagnosed with attention deficit disorder, yet somehow all of these items remain tucked inside... many of them rusted, bent, folded, gouged, chewed, broken, torn and/or lovingly mutilated. enter at your own risk.

blank pages.

(i never write on the first page.
it's bad luck bad luck bad luck.)

darkness. small insects. flying things. plastic wheels.
cracks of sunlight. blueberry stains.
a feather. an old elastic,
banding nothing together.

photos of you. sketches of your kitchen, your garden.
to-do lists. a scrap of cloth from your favourite old shirt.
grease from a grilled cheese sandwich.

sylvia's cell phone number. police reports.
old movie stubs. a subway transfer from runnymede station.
morse code. a swedish flag.
shopping lists. postcards from florence and marseilles.
loneliness.

laurel leaves. rose petals. bread crusts.
orange peels. potato skins. a popsicle stick.

fishing line. bird seed.
pink squirts from your lava lamp.
thorns.
smutty haiku. adhesive tape.
x-ray specs. cigarette smoke.
fear.
unnatural tendencies. denim.

black and white photos
from a camping trip: me with a sketchbook,
drawing the leaky blue canvas tent with your bucket hat
drying on the centre pole.

dog tags. rabbit ears. meditations. medications.
detours through madness. maps of winnipeg
and copenhagen. piano keys. a flattened hostess chip bag.
bicycle clips. barbed wire. a starbucks card.
three centennial $1 bills. a texaco star.
matchbooks from somebody's wedding. recipes
for vegetarian soup stock. deadlines for submissions.
ideas for a garbage collage. handlebar streamers from my blue
eaton's glider. the rusted bumper from my first car.

baseball cards from alpha-bits boxes.
irving layton's autograph.
a.y. jackson's autograph.
guy lafleur's autograph.
a ferron guitar pick
and a coaster from the dover hotel.

playbills from the sidetrack café
an ashtray from ponderosa steakhouse
draft glasses nicked from duffy's tavern
a small white piece of the parthenon
given to me by jen spencer after a school trip to greece

my aunt verna's poodle pin.
a button from carol's dress uniform.
my mom's thimble.
her recipe for gingersnaps
and a nugget from her wedding band
with the words "for always"
still legible. dad's paintbrushes and pipe cleaners.

my little brother's blue soccer jersey.
my big brother's onion gum and rolling papers.
beeswax candles from tofino. snowflakes.
a bistro praha receipt for fried cheese & lager.

turquoise.
goldenrod.
bubbles.
smooth edges.
rough language.
intimacies.
windows.
top-secret blueprints.
goldfish.
a lock of my true love's hair.

(prompt: William Stafford, "What's in my journal")

homo for the holidays

thanksgiving 1975
uncle mac disapproves of my shirt
– not because it's army surplus,
but because it has american stripes on the shoulders.
damned yankees. think they own everything.

my mom just plain disapproves.
it's thanksgiving, why can't you wear a dress? she yells..
it's thanksgiving, why can't i
play football with the boys? i yell back,
slamming the door behind me.

thanksgiving 1983
ross has heard about my trip
to provincetown with jane.
queers still have the run of the place?
he wants to know. i want to know how he knows;
how he happened to visit there
in the '60s with his best friend kevin. twice.
i want to know what happened to kevin.

easter 1986
davy wants to know
about that rumour in high school.
all those kids thought you and jenny were queer.
well, guess what, little brother: jenny and i
never even kissed.
she got married; said i should, too.
she started having babies; said it was something she always
wanted to do
(even more than to live in a castle in Scotland
with me...)
and your sister? well, davy,
your sister started sleeping with women; discovered it was
something she always wanted to do.

solstice 1993
steve's fiancée has taken work in the states.
no jobs for nurses in canada, his mother sneers.
it's so horrible. she has to work on an AIDS floor. she says she doesn't mind,
but that's just awful, don't you think?
i mean, it serves them right, don't you think?
because those people … pretty much …
bring it on themselves ... don't you think?

those people.
i do not bother to inform her that some of those people are
sitting at her kitchen table
... that i am one of *those people.*

samhain 1996
my second cousin hasn't seen me in three years.
did you know that i'm not married any more?
she declares – as if it were some kind of an achievement,
like quitting smoking.

i want to grab her and shake her, and shout,
neither am i!
annie – my lover, my best friend, love of my life,
my partner of nine years,
with whom i shared a house, two dogs
and a sport utility vehicle –
my beloved annie has left me,
and i'm
dying
inside.

but all i can tell her is,
i like what you've done
with your hair.

those of us

dedicated to all of those who, at a very early age,
realized they weren't given the same handbook
as everyone else when they were put on this planet

those of us who didn't like pink
those of us who had no time for dolls
those of us who preferred to climb trees
those of us who despised wearing dresses

those of us who wanted to be cowboys
those of us who chose bikes over barbie
those of us who didn't couldn't wouldn't fit inside the box
those of us who felt strangled by lace

those of us who could outrun the boys
those of us who never seemed to get it
those of us who felt the disconnect
those of us who couldn't ever quite say why

those of us whose nails were never polished
those of us whose hair was too damn short
those of us who didn't know our place
those of us who *throw pretty good for a girl*

those of us who smoked and swore
those of us who dared to swagger
those of us who drank to resist
those of us who said *fuck it* and kissed

those of us who slow-danced in shadows
those of us whose passions you fear
those of us who live in denial
those of us who are bent/twisted/queer

those of us who are told we are freaks
those of us who are told we are broken
those of us who are told to conform
those of us badgered with *why won't you try?*

those of us who are tortured with secrets
those of us who don't ask and can't tell
those of us who are bashed out of "decency"
those of us who are told *god hates fags/burn in hell*

those of us who dare to be different
those of us who live right next door
those of us who make your husband nervous
those of us who like it that way

are more like you than you will ever know

corbett hall

banff centre, science residence, before the artists moved in

prior to the invasion of the poets, these walls had to endure:
constraint programming belief revision
          and combinatorial optimization
symmetry and bifurcation in biology
quantum mechanics on the large scale
cumulative algebra and geometry
recent developments in string theory
statistical mechanics of polymer mode
recent advances in algebraic and enumerative
          combinatorics
differential invariants and invariant differential equations
defects and their dynamics and localization behaviour
          in reaction-diffusion systems and applications
          to the natural sciences
galaxy formation: a herculean challenge (!)
and
applicable harmonic analysis

then the writers came.

they brought wild rice, dark coffee,
australian wine and strawberries;
green tea and dog-eared copies of mary oliver
and leonard cohen, pablo neruda and billy collins,
william carlos williams.

they brought pages soaked in blood, extra blankets,
their daughters' tears and their own string theory,
which is that you should always carry some
in your backpack
in case you run out of safety pins, trail mix,
rhyming couplets or distraction retardant.

the writers stared out the windows at the deer.
wapiti walked through their dreams
to the thrum of the bow valley heartbeat.
they replaced lab measurements with metaphor.
their lone nod to harmonic analysis
consisted of singing *happy birthday* to a dear friend
to celebrate forty years of being awed by this blessed earth.

they laughed. they wept. they wrote.
they swam, they skied, and laughed and wrote some more
and when they believed they could no longer move the pen
across the page
they wrote more still – by sunlight, by candlelight
by the light of a three sisters moon.
they went deep.
they lost themselves in the mountain peaks
they lost themselves in the blank page
and got back out alive.

they listened to their mothers
and left the place in better condition
than they had found it.

melanoma

you have marked me
not like a bruise, not like a scar
carved by the blade of a knife
or the cruel razor cuttings of comparison
more like a tiny mole on my skin,
not born of the womb but
appearing years later, mysteriously
from a soft, hidden place
where the blue-black of cobalt meets the weight of lead
in a spot you cannot see without a mirror
like the nape of the neck, the small of the back
the top of the back of the thigh

it's old now, isn't it, this hot and dark thing between us
no longer a slow fire or a gradual scald
more like a jolt of live current
metal on hot screeching metal
and for the first time i wonder who it is you see
when you light the first lamp
now that your hands no longer scorch me

you have marked me
i mistook the rumpled coat and dishevelled hair
as signs of tortured genius
turns out you were just a slob with an endearing smile
the string of unmade beds should have been my first clue

and now i know my childhood ended
on that day you stopped me from drowning
and who could blame me for falling
and who could blame you for not

so now i wake up screaming
no time left for bargaining
no way to ever satisfy your appetite for sad, small things

you have marked me
and i wish i could escape the crush of it

wish it didn't still burn me up at night
wish i could turn this searing wound into something benign and casual,
a harmless crusted scab that i could absently pick at
until it heals over or falls off ...

but there will never be any denying
the malignant consequence of you

indelirium

she is tired of whiling away her afternoons
writing espresso-fuelled sonnets in dark, arty cafés
where formica and incense clash,
where forks are caked with snot-dried yolk
from the morning's egg and bacon rasher
where cigarette smoke makes her long to put her mouth
on something besides a bottomless cup of lukewarm brown.

she wants to possess things she cannot own
she would like to sentence to death
– or would that be life –
the slippery, fetid, two-pronged words
from which she cannot hide.

she would like to eradicate television
save the infidels from the internet
blow up every blackberry on the planet.

there are times she would like to simply disappear,
shave her head
jump off a bridge
burn her own skin

she worries about the disappearing bees
she worries about the northern seas
and whether she's had too much fair-trade sumatra today

she wonders: if warhol had a cell phone,
what ringtone would he program it to?
and she wonders about those bees, are the bees
getting through?
have the disappearing worker bees
been secretly slaving away for you?

are you getting any REM sleep, greenland?

she'd like to know if a trickle of apologetic rhetoric
will be currency enough
to delay the global drowning,
satisfy the american idolatry,
force-feed the gluttony,
finance the transparent liberty
that is trans-fattening the rest of us
while causing you, greenland, to, inexplicably,
shrink

and you, you by the windowpanes
she needs you to know
the women are not talking about michelangelo

we are talking about acid rain and child soldiers
we are talking about our mothers' tumours
and our daughters' fears
we talk about the false that becomes true
we discuss the lie that becomes you

yes, we dare!
yes, yes, we dare!
we dare to put our fingers there!
our gin-soaked, progesterone-stoked trigger fingers
used to care
and yes, she wants you to know that we still do
but the bees and the polar bears are no longer there

the women are not talking of michelangelo
we are trying not to show our fear
we are pondering how long we have
before the dancing foxes
the hummingbirds
and all the tender kisses
disappear

the knowing

I.

i went mad
let the morning come
i went away
let the evening come
i went astray
let the river run
i went within
let the winter dark begin
i went to the well
sound the living bell
i went to the drum
let the dancers come
i turned to the northern sky
let the dreamers fly
i left my body
let the spirit rise
my eyes went black
bring the madness back

II.

i want to tell you about the knowing
but the weight of this sorcery is suffocating

i want to tell you about the knowing
but it too often leads to the leaving

i want to tell you about the knowing
but you are there and i am here
and we've come this far without naming it

i want to tell you about the knowing
but will the telling – under the sun
under the moon
under the wild purple flame of night –
bring us any closer to peace?

i want to tell you about the knowing
about the cedars
the scotch pine
the osprey
the elk
about the shell shaped like a heart
the mountain's raging thirst.
i want to tell you
about the athabasca
the north saskatchewan
the bow / the red

i want to tell you
about the third eye
the medicine wheel
the rose quartz
the monkey's paw

i tried to tell you about
the crossing over
the deluge
the quicken
the release

i couldn't tell you about
the pomegranate
the sacred circle
the voices
the drownings

i need to tell you, sisters and brothers,
about the knowing
but first i must tell you about
the burning

getting back

you can get there from here:
from a dime-store notebook
from a coffee-stained, second-hand table
through a tiny, stained-glass window
above the dishes in the kitchen sink

you can get there from a bad dream
from a summer storm
from a fork in the road
from a backseat that smells like bourbon and guilt
you can get there from your treehouse
from your grandmother's easter ham and onions
from the smell of brylcreem in your brother's hair
from the small of your lover's back

you can get there from an old love letter
from granddad's hand-rolled cigarettes
from touching the shiny pages of the eaton's catalogue
from fingering the spools of thread in mama's sewing box.
sometimes you can get there from the 99th street diner
from the rainbow bar at closing time
from a latte at the sugar bowl cafe
from the pipe tobacco smell forever woven into your dad's
favourite sweater

you can navigate the crown of sagittarius
through the tip of orion's sword
follow snakes into woods shimmering with silver lichen,
take a left at van gogh's ear and hang a right
just past carcajou
lose your map and compass at montana joe's full-serve
you can get there in a red canoe
on a dragonfly's wing
in a fast car with the top down
in a rusty old john deere

you might be led astray by a crisp white shirt
seduced by a pixie with felt slippers and a flute
by a magician with a recipe book
by the scent of strawberries
you might miss the signs and fall off a cliff
ignore your better judgement and accept a ride
from a pompous bore
you might detour through marriage, catastrophe,
through a decade of drinking, prison or neglect

you might allow yourself to be distracted
by shiny baubles, the promise of prairie skies
even let yourself become lazy, heavy, indifferent, sad
and still, still ... still you can get there from here

back to your emerald self,
to the promise of the blank page,
to the calm of morning light after centuries of dark
to that unfinished shade of newborn first-breath green

when they come for me

when they come for me the first time
i won't be here. i'll be dressing the poem up in leather
and taking it out to the bar, one last time.
twirling it round the dance floor,
pressing it up against the bathroom door
caressing its ear, nuzzling its cheek,
biting its pouty lower lip
insinuating my leg between its thighs and
buying it one last drink
before deciding
i need to go home alone.

when they come for me for real,
i'll be wearing cowboy boots / a green hat / and no drawers

when they question me
i will speak nothing but the truth ... except when i lie
which will be convincingly / and often

when they feed me
i won't clean my plate
i will eat somebody's words
i will make coffee out of brittle bones
and stone soup out of blank stares

when they inject me
i will not resist / i will merely offer my arm
and pray they leave no marks

when they imprison me
i will not notice. i will find the one chink in the wall
where the light gets in
and allow it gradually to blind me

when they hang me
i will forgive the rope.

when they bury me
i will not stick around for long
because dirt is messy and if it rains, mucky.
and because i got places to go, and when i said i needed
grounding
i sure didn't mean six feet under, sister.
no, when they bury me, i'll send a stand-in, i'll look on from over
someone's shoulder
and listen to what they have to say about my dearly departed self

when they eulogize me
i hope they will laugh ...
i intend to.

when they dig me up, years and possibly centuries
from now,
they will find precious little left.
because i intend to tunnel out and about
and become one with the night-diggers ...
who shall elect me queen of the mole people and grant me
everlasting life.

just when they've almost forgotten me
they'll remember me,
miss me, curse me, sanitize me, redeem me,
forgive me, ask forgiveness of me, delete me
and throw me back in the hole.

when i haunt their dreams, they'll wish they had
treated me better.

when they hear me rattling around their halls at night
they'll tell themselves it's just the wind

when they finally go to wash the blood off their hands
and discover it's all their own,
they will find another way to blame it on the muslims
or the jews
or the catholics or the serbs
or the irish or the goths
or the poets or the queers
or the methodists or the phone company
or the avian flu or the west nile
or the third reich or the banks

and then they'll just go back to blaming it all
on the mothers

she had a way

i had a way of articulating my pain and it was clumsy.
she had a way of putting her hands on me …
and it was good.
she put her hands on many people,
and she had a way about it ...
but the way she put her hands on a woman
was different from the way she put her hands on a man.

she had a way of gently placing her hands
on the back of my neck and rubbing out my soreness.
she had a way of moving energy around under my skin
that steered me through colours and light
(which was merely, according to Science,
photo-electrical impulses
detonating gently behind my gullible eyelids).
she had a way of tolerating science.

she had a way of putting her hands on my womanly body
that made me feel safe, drunk, and dizzy
she had a way of putting her hands on a tired, aching,
tension-filled rock pile of flesh that made it stop hurting.

she had a way of handling a body of women.
she had a way of honouring a body of women's work.
she had a healing way of putting her hands on a woman …
without scorching

she had a way of pulling her own aches and pains
out of the body of a woman.
she had a way of concealing her woman's body
in the hands of a man.

she had a way of wanting to be held by a body of women.
she had a wanton way of wanting warm women
she found wanting

she had a womonly way of wanting
bodies of fallen women.
she had the body of a wishful womon falling way behind.
she had a way of not wanting a man's hands
touching her tenderly.
she had a womon's way of handling wimmin's hands
on her body.
she had a witchy way of capturing a womon's body
without using her hands.

she had a definite way with women.

she had a way of putting her words in women's mouths.
she had a guarded way with women's hands
on her own body.
she handed over her body to women who were handy
she had a way of gazing longingly at other women's hands.
she had a woman's hands
and a man's way of shoving them into her pockets.
she had a way of sticking her hands
in other women's business.
she had a way of putting her hands
on other women's women.

she had a way of having her way with me, hands down.
she had a way of feeding me, hand to mouth
she had a way of bleeding me
she had a way of putting her blessed hands
on my half-hearted, hard-as-nails heart and healing me.
she had a heavenly way of putting her words and mine
on air
she had a hellish way of starting fires
with her hot, hot hands

she had a sway … she had a way …
she had a way of putting her hands on a woman.

correction lines

oh mom
it's been too long
still lookin for some kind of redemption
still achin for goodnight kisses
for one soft night of calm
in a warm flannel sheet

oh mom
all around me
i see love
i see love but it's not raw it's convoluted and
still all about conquerin

oh mom, sure wish you could call to say hi
but not on a blackberry
no use for them
lots better things to do
with these restless thumbs

oh mom
yeah of course i'm still learnin
oh yeah me i'm still workin through
this aversion to life
lessons you tried to tell, truths you hoped
i'd come to know
when i was backstreet smug and not too attentive
like don't put your mouth on cold metal
don't ever take more than you need
don't fake tears or kindness
don't fear an occasional detour
through the broken roads of lonesome county
and always trust your heart
to the correction lines

oh ma
the young ones here are still searchin & hopeful
still desperate to channel ginsberg & cobain & plath
the reckless still line up for night rides
with jimmy dean & brando
pissed and far too clever
for housework or baseball

and me, i'm scavengin long-stemmed intimacies
like a magpie
drawn to junky things that shine

and twilight is still hard for me
but don't worry
y'know i'm turnin out OK
in my own little slow-burnin
metaphorical kind of way

and oh mom i almost forgot
i met a girl / we went out
supper was two wines
and a big rock
oh mom / she broke my heart
and how much would it matter
if she was the one?

oh mom
oh mom
how can i begin to tell a god you never believed in
how much i miss you today

where have all the watering holes gone?

poet returns to the scene of the crimes

the queens is still there
the yank long gone, bulldozed into condos
sometime last century
happy hour at the wellington just went up in smoke ...
and duffy's clarkson gave way to tiffs sports bar
where there's creemore springs on the pull now
and labatt's 50 stubbies are a distant memory

first forbidden kiss
in that dingy hotel bathroom
don't you ever knock? i'm trying to pee
who knew one fleeting fiery touch could change a life

knobby and ronny gone to barfly heaven
and tess now a permanent fixture at the simcoe,
living on beer and onion sandwiches, the last-call diehards
hoping she doesn't fall down the stairs on her way up to bed
every night

pool table and cigarette machine also gone, replaced by
video games and flat-screen tvs
joey used to know us all by what we drank:
a blue, an ex, two rye-and-waters, four pints of draft
and a couple bags of humpty dumpty chips for the table
and how are you tonight ladies? didja win your big game?

she's serving down at the diner now,
tips nowhere near as good
but run outta the bar by younger, hipper, tighter waitstaff
now all pierced and rude and working three jobs
to pay for their dye jobs and cell phone time

the grandfathers still fish off the rocky shore
smooth casts with long rods; it never was about
how much they caught

and squawking gulls still bully cold fries
and sandwich crusts out of the chubby hands
of crying toddlers at centennial beach

sun-splintered middle-class runabouts tied up at the dock:
the boats get replaced but the tacky nautical names
never seem to evolve: *sea breeze*, *best kept secret*,
hannah's joy, *weekend bliss*
almost killed myself
skidding into the back of a sailboat called *mary*
one drunken night after baseball
and spinner the only one around
to make sure i got home okay
that spinner – who else could go into the bar
with two bucks, tell tall tales all night
and come out six beers full
with four bucks in her jacket pocket –
and whatever happened to her anyway?

five points still the hub of the downtown, eh
quieter though, if it's possible – city three times larger
but urban core dying
eviscerated by the big box shopping hell on tower hill

the bay still a glistening emerald
if you can see past the burger king signs, bus station fumes
constant construction bunging up the shoreline

no more disney afternoons on dunlop street, either
now it's punk shows at the roxy, lap dances at the imperial
beef on a bun and french onion soup
finally bumped off the menu
at the town & country steakhouse
first by nachos and caesar salads, then guacamole
and sushi,

now it's tabouli – what the hell's tabouli? the oldtimers grump –
and something called a triple-goddamn
skim-milk-decaf latté
hey, remember that time harris sent kate and me out
to take pictures of people looking up at the eclipse?

sorry, boss. nobody cared what was happening
in the simcoe county sky that day,
but we did get a great shot
of a buckin'-horse hood ornament
on a flashy new pickup truck next to us at a traffic light
and that's about when we decided
to kick-start our weekend early
with pitchers of molsons out at the horseshoe valley lounge
descending into the soft grey of another fuzzy friday night
not taking photos of eclipse-watchers
or howling at the moon,
just gettin' happy drunk
and comparing notes on who we'd slept with

and harris never did ask why we didn't come back
to the office
or demand to see our photos
musta figured we needed to blow off some steam:
coupla small-town weekly newspaper girls
growing restless
and horny for danger

oh yeah, those were the days

skillet prayers & polar bears

I.

we were never ones to kneel at bedsides
or in dark, quiet closets
in my house prayers clacked out of typewriter keys
splashed out of burbling coffee pots
leaked indiscriminately from burning eyes when we chopped onions

our prayers were not always cries for help
sometimes they were tattered love letters
fingers drumming on a table
kites on the wind, heard by the wrong gods

many years ago, our prayers danced in cast-iron skillets
sizzling with butter and garlic and earthy greens.
seasoned by the alchemy of the grandmothers,
their heft almost too much for one hand,
those trusted pans were as sacred as rosaries:

dear god, let there be enough eggs
let there be rain for the crops
let our boys come home safe ...
& dear god, keep our husbands away from rye whiskey
and loose women
and the race track.
amen.

ah, the prayers that were said over those hot pans ...
they crackled and hissed with smoking hot lard
but they always smelled like
hope

II.

we had our skillet prayers too, you and i
but they were all shallow and selfish back then
back when we thanked god for slow-dances
and sweet lemon gin
and we were held tightly / but not together
by part-time boyfriends
back when every skillet prayer was a jackpot
and we were forever falling, in love
and into tall, smouldering grasses
wearing puka shells and earth shoes
and our john lennon glasses

not that many years later, a shy thin girl
spelled out your name in seedlings
during a parched summer of tree-planting
and clove cigarettes
come twilight your hands built campfires
fed more prayers into the skillet
called on the grandmothers
to bless the scorched earth with rain

and when the rains did come
you zipped your sleeping bags together
shared thermos dregs in a sweltering tent with leaky walls
read to each other from steamy novels
drank bad wine and kissed like blazes

eventually she came to know
that things connected to you seldom take root
still, somewhere out there
you can read your name in a stand of wood
or at least you could
until that boreal tinderbox went up in flames
in a summer of endless wildfires trumped, ironically,
by a merciless wall of water
in a city that care forgot
and skillet prayers could not reach

III.
in an earlier, verdant time,
when you and i were mere saplings ourselves,
we marched to stop the nukes / to save the whales
to keep songbirds in the sky / and the wetlands wet
but we were reckless with the bears.
we were reckless with a lot of things back then:
reckless with love, and the sun and our skin
reckless with water, soil, the thickening air

whatever we needed, we just sent up another skillet prayer
it was never our intention to drown the great northern bear

we laughed when janis asked the lord
to buy her a mercedes benz;
now it's SUVs and hummers
the wish list never ends

the grandmothers tried to warn us

long before things started really heating up
the grandmothers peered into their skillets
and saw flames at the top of the world
now the white bears aren't the only ones on thin ice
the top of the world is on fire
the ice caps are melting
the polar bears are drowning
and our grandchildren are the ones in the pan

and the grandmothers ...
the grandmothers continue to kneel
over their humble, heavy, healing skillets
they hold the prayers
hold the love
hold the heat and blood of the world
in their blessed, healing hands ...
they always
always have.

LAURIE MACFAYDEN grew up in southern Ontario and has lived in Edmonton since 1984. She spent 30 years as a sports journalist, most recently at the *Edmonton Journal*. She left the news media in June 2007 to focus on her own writing and visual arts projects. This is her debut collection of poetry.

A painter, photographer and avid traveller, Laurie is a frequent performer on the Raving Poets' open-mic stage in Edmonton. She is a member of the Writers Guild of Alberta, Edmonton's Stroll of Poets, the Edmonton Arts Council and the Visual Arts Alberta Association. She blogs at http://spatherdab.wordpress.com and her art lives at www.lauriemacfayden.com